Valentine

Ruth Maus

2019 FINALIST
The Birdy Poetry Prize
by Meadowlark Books

Valentine

POEMS
Ruth Maus

A MEADOWLARK BOOK

Meadowlark (an imprint of Chasing Tigers Press)
meadowlark-books.com
P.O. Box 333, Emporia, KS 66801

Copyright © 2019 Ruth Maus

All rights reserved. This book or any portion thereof
may not be reproduced or used in any manner whatsoever
without the express written permission of the author
except for the use of brief quotations in a book review.

Cover Image by Ruth Maus
Interior illustrations by Ruth Maus

ISBN: 978-1-7322410-7-7

Library of Congress Control Number: 2019943942

To the poetry in all sentient beings.

Acknowledgments

We arrive at this stage of our lives only through the nurturing and support of so many, so thank you—to my mother and father, who read us all those nursery rhymes and stories, loved reading, and remained forever curious; to my brothers with love, to my absolutely wonderful favorite nephew for his artistic encouragement, to my outstanding and loyal friends on several continents; and to the Topeka, Washburn University, and Smith College poet communities. Many thanks to my excellent poetry teachers Eric McHenry, Richard Wilbur, and William Van Vorris, to Creative Writing instructor Michael Gorra, and to Roy Beckemeyer, Sandra Beasley, and Janet Jenkins-Stotts. Special gratitude goes to the beloved animal companions of my life—you have slept by my side, carried me through happy meadows and over hurdles, tolerated my shortcomings, and shed constantly. Namaste to Edith Maus, Shinzen Young, Andrew Schauer, and Verla Dick for your gifts—love, serenity, and understanding of the big picture. Also many thanks to Tracy Million Simmons at Meadowlark Books and Kevin Rabas for taking a chance on me, and to the editors of the following magazines, e-zines, and journals for publishing my poems:

Inscape: "Hurricane Dance," "The Center of It All," "Guerilla Warfare"

Grecourt Review: "Native Stone"

Lighten Up Online: "Cat Tale"

Orchards Poetry Journal: "Brexit"

The poem "Ars Poetica" received recognition in the Kansas Authors Club Literary Contest-2018, Theme category

"Preservative" was posted on the Facebook page of Great Lakes Hospice in Topeka, Kansas

Blessings to you all.

Contents

Dawn in the Land of Odds

Dawn in the Land of Odds 3
The Big Chill 4
The Sun Worshippers 5
Humpty 6
Path 7
Velveeta Poetica 8
Moon Poem 9
Fall Bloom 10
Persuasion (In Three Acts) 11
Waking in the Pink 12
Ars Poetica 13
Dusting 14
One Day While Driving 15
Solstice 16
Modern Love Story 17
The Center of It All 18
Last Tango in D.C. 20
Communities 21
The Plumber 22
Another Existential Dilemma 23
The Thinker 24
Curriculum Vitae 25

Preservative

Preservative 29
When Lizards Dream 31
A Tart's Rouge 32
Plenipotentiary Poker 33
Whitey's Bar 34
Tranquility Base 35
Cultivation 36
Maybe Take A Stand 37
Crusoe, On The Verge 38
M. H. 40

Stay by My Cradle, Please 41
Illegals 42
Brexit 43
Homage 44
The Lot Sent to Munich 45
The Garden 46
Cat Tale 47
Each Life Could Be 48
When the Aliens Finally Reveal Themselves 50
Throwaway People 51
The Guardian 52
The Blue Potomac Waltz 54
Pinkie 55
Native Stone 56
The Second Time Climbing Teotihuacán 58
Evidence 59

Dove Season

Dove Season 63
Waking Up Shocking Pink 64
Guerilla Warfare 65
Halloween 66
Disclaimer 67
Spotlight on a Mummer 68
Blue Bandage 69
Allen Ate the Earring 71
The Brother 72
To Sit Around Fires 73
It Depends on Your Perspective 74
Hurricane Dance 76
Or Possibly the Queen of Lazy 77
Poem for Poetry Geeks 78
The Convenience Store Clerk 80
Parts of a Hen 81
The Pusher 82
Todd rode by 86
Valentine 87
Ars (Not Quite) Poetica 88

Notes 91
A Note About the Author 97

Dawn in the Land of Odds

Dawn in the Land of Odds

You're one red mitten calling to its mate, one hellcat with a repo'd Harley. You're an orphaned eight ball, now an oddball, and a single tooth that finally fell from a baby's mouth, like a short fall from slobbery grace. You're the only mouse wily enough to evade the trap that caught The Stupid Ones in its cold clench. You're the encrypted password that can't be cracked, the spook that haunts the radical cathedral. You're one vanity beyond beauty and one shiver past any comfort.

It's all You.

Ah, but welcome to our land, to the sideshow where you're one of us and just as keen. Come, claim a homestead, pick a spot, and build a camp on this prime real estate. Swear allegiance and play your new national anthem in the open air at dawn, one tentative note at a time on your tinny harmonica. Someday soon your repo will be replaced by a Bronco. Your harmonica will swell to a calliope, in harmony, screaming *Dust In the Wind* or *Livin' La Vida Loca* and you will fit right in. Welcome, friend, to America. Here you will be proud to build fences out of bottle caps, or to stun a moose with a bean-bag gun.

The Big Chill

They say
the Greenland icecap is melting away
right before our eyes. But Greenland isn't green
and most of us gawkers get stuck between
Could it be true? and nearsighted dismay
over what to do.

I say
let's go to Greenland while it still
isn't green, as if we had planned it that way,
hoping to beat the shillers and doomsday
prophets before the pervasive obnoxious chill
gets warm
and green in Greenland becomes the noxious norm.

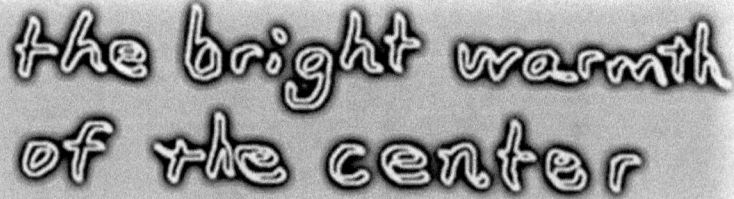

The Sun Worshippers

At the pool the bronzed assemble,
greased and horizontal, in a
bake-off of burnt offerings to
their temperamental god.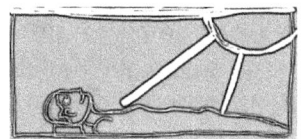

Flesh and flesh and little snips of
cloth held up by love and Lycra.
Sweat bakes to musk, a baste and
a crust over muscles and muttony
thighs. Brown to a blush, never a
blister. Time to turn over on the
concrete altar.

Someday soon a little cancer cloud
will unfold like a serviette, like an
origami of sepia doom, as the sacrifices
and brute faith are consumed.

But today, the righteousness of salt
on a monster margarita sings
psalm and hallelujah enough.

Humpty

When Humpty Dumpty took the infamous great fall, did it ever
occur to anyone that maybe Humpty was a girl? And the fact
that Humpty's scrambled brain couldn't get her act together,
showing predilections, as she did, for high places, doesn't make

her an egg either. Rather, and with a name like Humpty
it's hard not to assume this, I believe she was "fallen" in
more ways than one. Probably a naïve and roundish country
girl who came to the big city, in this case gossipy London,

to get a tattoo of Lynyrd Skynyrd, and instead sadly
rolled her dumpty over easy with all the king's men.
But by then young Humpty had cracked up so badly
her sunny side clouded and she rotted in a looney bin.

Reassembly, of course, was impossible to be found:
no savory out of sulphury; no wholesome from unsound.

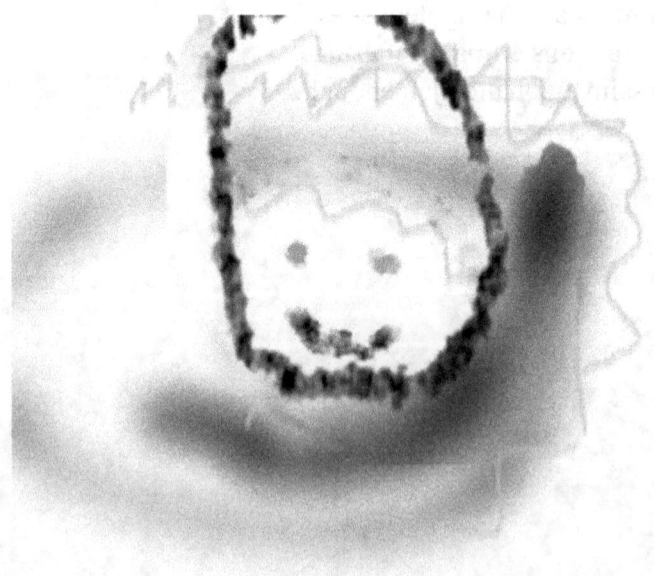

Path

Puffed from the raw materials you bring,
you'll chase a noisy life of luck and thrill,
zigzagging and embracing everything,

not knowing you're a leaden human being –
all fat blood, lust, and dirt, strained through goodwill –
not trusting the redeeming ace you bring.

You'll chase the giggle of a flirty spring,
but wolves compete to skin you out. They kill
each lovely random pleasure, everything.

So plead with all the gods worth worshipping
to fortify your wisdom, lest some shrill
tribunal gauge the character you bring,

or worse, your own ill-nature's heavy sting
envenoms any brief reprieve. No skill
can shield the reckless death of everything.

Through journeys of a thousand steps you cling
to the uneven path of life until
it ends, then you surrender what you bring,
enfolded in the greater Everything.

Velveeta Poetica

That Buddhist girl who skates roller derby
carries bite marks on her soul. She orates
with the primal syntax of a recovering hillbilly,
as in, "I got to get out of this P.O.S. hole,"
and dines on Dairy Queen swirls, blood
thinners, and melted cheese. Compatibly,
her stomach twangs the ringtone of the
1812 Overture, with cannons roaring.

She told me she wanted to sneak up on
God. I pointed out that God is everywhere,
making Him or Her difficult to lap, jam,
or block. Her explanation had something
to do with some friend's kosher marijuana.
(Who knew?) But when she saw she was
losing me she turned the tables, asking,
"May I offer you some Gouda?"

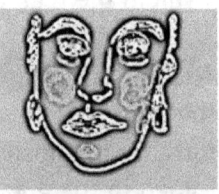

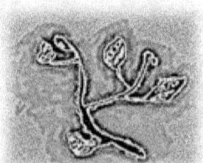

Moon Poem

The moon, like a stony hanger-on,
pulls on us like a suckling child, its
demands too impertinent to ignore: tide
in, tide out, light on, light
out, and always
look up.

Fall Bloom

Red remorse
to wash
from your anvil fists.
My blood, My Dear, my
face.

Sweetly
new pulpy blossoms
swell. Fluid flowers
that hurt like hell.

I bloom
down the beaten path
in seasoned disarray,
as flesh and promises
decay.

Persuasion (In Three Acts)

Dawn disturbed by desperados,
two master actors cast as commandos
whose poleax paws and stiff appendages
thunder-gallop-slam my tenderest, fullest, sleepiest places.

Shrieking "Judas Priest!" I stumble
to feed them organ meats and kibble,
our morning comic opera's crescendo:
the plumpish prima donna, foiled, swearing in *falsetto*.

The *coda*, according to their libretto,
a Duet For Declawed Outlaws *bel canto;*
then bow with high-fives and imperious glances—
though I can't be certain when only half-awake
without my glasses.

Waking In The Pink
To R. L.

The night shift cook, a vo-tech grad,
exits the cooler cold and blue,
another paunchy deadbeat dad
whose shift is through.

The fog is vaguely curious,
The way day breaks at Grape & Grill.
This is his house, his terminus,
a gin mill.

He flips off Stanley at the bar
with realpolitik and nerve,
for bragging of his Bronze Star.
What purpose does it serve?

What use his poems or his flan?
Both rubbery with little joy,
the whimpers of a bogeyman,
once an altar boy.

He notices a screwball dame
settling in to drink her fate.
Recalls how his ex-wife became
twice his weight.

He pauses, orders ginger ale,
a shaky twinkle finds his face,
and signals her a fresh cocktail,
just in case.

Maybe the day will not be blue,
distracted by this sticky flower.
He'll see what his pick-up lines will do.
Give it an hour.

Ars Poetica

A poem is a careless beau
whose charm and charge won't let us go,
an egoist that pulls us in
to seize our brass, again, again.

So poems and their traps collude,
with loveliness and attitude,
to strut themselves through bone and steel
and snip our hearts with their appeal,

to flash like heat on waxy milk,
sometimes scalding, sometimes silk,
then stir their words and recombine
in poems that make the stars align.

Some liberated poems set free
a hip hop riff, a rhapsody,
as winding, wounding, slams, or blues,
they jazz us any way they choose;

they woo us with their fine designs,
all rosy-cheeked and bouncing lines;
or birthed with forceps, bruised with sin,
reflect our ringworm-riddled twin,

whose naked verse beguiles with pain,
who bleeds out from the jugular vein,
whose life and death demand a voice.
As if the poet had a choice.

And when delivered straight to God,
these words, both grandiose and flawed,
a multiflora rose of rhymes,
to pray, to pray a thousand times.

Dusting

In the storage unit labeled *A-1, For Sanity's Retention*, he bolts grief away with a large hard padlock. Outside, he waits for his unskillfulness to ripen, for pieces to be picked up and handles to be gotten on things. Maybe then, he tells himself.

The dust on the coffee table mocks him, "If you were a better person there would have been tears, or one of those counseling groups, also involving tears."

"Yes," he writes in the dust.

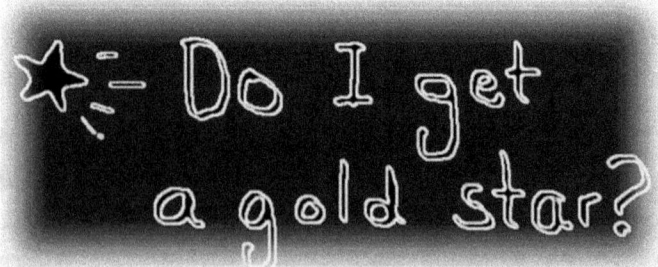

One Day While Driving

One day while driving
I saw
herds of umbrellas
crossing the plains of a rainy intersection.

Two by two
they had paired themselves,
guided by some subconscious imprint
of an earlier Deluge.

Solstice

When
spring finally
limps in,
untangling winter's
knots of leaden woolens
and clotted theorems,
I unwrap striates of rose and
honeysuckle, perfume and pollen, the guileless
timelessness of ripe sky. In the new grass I barefoot a
hornpipe dance with my old toes and cartwheel to the squeaks
and thunders of croakers cheeky for love. I share the honeyed
nectar of clover buds with the bees, happy and busy.
Lightning bugs wink, proliferating in the twilight
like overconfident kisses, inviting more, more.
Then, the baby bunnies disassemble, the
wrens shutter whitewashed houses
in the maple, and gradually a
drubbing on the glass of a
soulless barometer,
as again, we
wither.

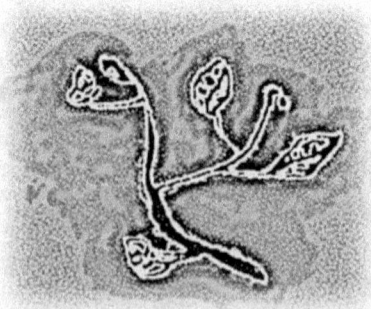

Modern Love Story   *

Gladys Thong wore her underwear way
too tight, but try as she might to lose
weight she remained a size twenty-eight.

Her boyfriend Jose had something to
say. "Baby, my Snuggle Buffalo, to
get you up requires a backhoe."

But Gladys was in no mood for his
judgmental attitude. "Oh poo," she said.
"And *you* have a tiny, pointed head.

"So if you're gonna be whiny let's both
call it quits, 'cause as girlfriends go, I'm
as good for you as it gets."

And so they parted, two odd ducks, both
broken-hearted, each seeking someone
else more deluxe.

However Gladys and Jose weren't really
that bizarre, because love, like underwear,
will only stretch so far.

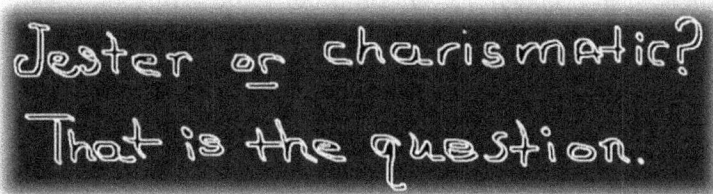

The Center of It All   *

The invalid mother is a big responsibility. And I am
the lone guardian. This does not explain my neurosis,
however, as I was a mess already. Who am I kidding?
I am Mother Teresa, a surefire candidate down the
compassionate path of sainthood—and hell, I'm not even
Catholic. I am some kind of artist,

or I teach tricks to housecats who would otherwise behave
like turnips. Sometimes I'm a cleaner of polypropylene
carpets, knowing what products take out what stains. Maybe
—just saying—I repackage the products in little plastic bottles
that I purchase for next to nothing at the dollar store and give
them away at dirty bus stops to dirty people. My guilty pleasure
would be redesigning the human body for maximum efficiency,
a Volvo's engineering, all redemptive and able to withstand

violence. We all die sometime. Maybe I am somebody who
measures capacity. We all have capacity. I could throw down
the gauntlet to those terrorists who confiscate it. I'm already
a terrorist myself at the center of it all. I know this because
I take charge in a crisis and because the numbers don't lie.
How many times have you been in the

hospital? But I am not who you think I am. I appear calm
when the hospice folks call to tell me of a new wound or
the need for pureed everything. I smile when dealing with
doctors and nurses and appointments and meds and special
compounded meds not covered by insurance. I purchase
the lift, the incontinence products, the wheelchair, all approved
with my excellent credit history. The expense like a chisel,
like groaning. Maybe I absorb the fat shitstorm of nursing
homes and Medicare. Even when I can never take a vacation
or a day off, life flattens like a midway of

nice manners. I have encountered a theory of unborn innocence. Actually I made it up, what with the lack of innocence and I'm pretty well born at this point. Maybe even old. It goes like this: why can we all help each other during a crisis, but after the soup and after the protoplasm and after the rosary, when the other drivers get behind the wheel everyone becomes rude? Honk if you are rude.

Last Tango in D.C.

Once you courted
me, attentive swain, all ardor
and peanut butter.

Teasing tango,
"Let's tango," lubricated passes
and long-stemmed roses.

"You and me, friend,"
(you wouldn't lie) "will now crescendo
in two-two tempo."

We rose up tux
and organdy, tongue and salt-juice skin,
torque and piston.

We whirled and moved the
world—or so we thought, tangled
and hot. Or maybe not.

Communities

Can tadpoles, with no obvious pectoral fins,
consider cocker spaniels and stockbrokers their twins?
Can the bishop embrace the turpentine and debris
from branches of roaches on his family tree?

If the village idiot were not our king of bones,
if our sharpened knives were plowshares, or rhinestones,
would happiness envelop all whose sentience
flows from the tributaries of connectedness?

Still, the old woman sweeps the floor of her hut and sighs
as the mare nickers for bran, or maybe French fries,
and crocodiles shed tears and repo men repossess,
and the universe wears a starry organza dress.

The Plumber

The faucet plunks a drip, drip, drip, that will
not stop, globbing the sink's active whiteness
with its compulsion for blank porcelain, running
up the water bill and wasting the sauce of life.
No amount of faucet tightening changes its mind,
as if the drip, once birthed, demands its fandango
in the course of plumbing civilizations, having
already plotted its spiral down the drain, down
the sewer, down the river to all the down places.

The arrival of my brother, however, with his
big boots and box of heavy tools, scares it into
arid submission. "What drip?" asks my brother
and I must admit all the power has shifted.

Where can I find a plumber as I drip my days
away, leaving fuddled nomadic spots and
evaporating my saucy life? Will I end up
in the down places too, or will some big
guerrilla with carbon-steeled, titanium-
carbide agility wrench me into the colorless
causeway where blemished is not an option?

Another Existential Dilemma

To focus, work, work harder and thus succeed
is the formula those who profess to know
would have us believe
is the way to go.

But despite our brilliant dedication
and gritty endeavors,
life hands us our guts and damnation
on a dirty platter. Whoever's

in charge of this karmic balancing scheme,
can you please re-calibrate the scale
so the stream
of the universe and I won't derail?

Let us blind pigs find
ample acorns. Let us know love and dodge cancer.
Let the cogs of the cosmos grind
out a genial answer

to whatever prayer we did or did not make.
And just in case,
let us know (for a lot's at stake)
what is earned, what is luck, and what is sloughed off grace.

The Thinker

A bronze well-muscled man sits chin in hand, alone, naked, and still.
Perhaps he's in a reverie, perhaps bound in servility, it's hard to tell.
Could be he's framing philosophy with his hard-flogged,
    half-fogged brain
and *that* is a strain.

Through mists, misfires, and mirrors, the man cogitates to try
to snag some useful magic daring enough to wander by.
A predatory sticky tongue, like a hungry wide-cast net,
his mind pursues such knowing, and occasionally he'll get
a sparkling gem amongst the little birds and tangled strings
to add to his collection of "the meaning of all things,"
to hoard these salient wisdoms promising they'll coalesce
into some Wow! enlightenment. Well . . . more or less.

But the homeliness of ignorance has affixed to the man's quest,
repelling easy answers to the questions he's addressed.
So when he's scorched his brain cells with a far-flung mental search,
gone through every oracle, hallucinogen, ivory tower, and church,
the thinker slowly devolves into helplessness and dread,
left hunched and waiting for—what?—
still holding up his head.

In a Paris museum garden sits this dumb and lovely creation
that cleverly Rodin produced to tease our rumination,
The Thinker prodding our thinking, keeping us guessing
    at all that he knows.
When maybe the thought that he's thinking is,
"Where the hell did I leave my clothes?"

Curriculum Vitae

If my uneven musings on a page
were faultless poems of artistry and style
whose words transcended nation, race, class, age,
called down the rain, cured ills, and for a while

displayed true courage, challenged evil thought,
provoked a revolution, belled the cat,
traversed the pirate seas with swag and swat,
rolled up the sunshine into butterfat,

if I could capture such indentured power
that lovers plucked my words to sway a heart,
and death postponed its rendezvous an hour,
and beauty bloomed while ugly fell apart,

then, despite my sins along the way,
"By God, she is a *poet*," they would say.

Preservative

Preservative

I have buried my dead in Topeka, the
formaldehyde for my memories. Of
itself Topeka is a medium falling out
of favor; but I still employ it to grasp
at a painfully artful resemblance of
what was once lovely.

My friends Babs, Buster Kitten, Sylvia,
Peaches, Jeff, King, Carambas, Clipper,
Gunther, Weasel, Sister, Amber, Kitty Boots,
Jose, Adolph, Bismarck, Georgie, Bubba,
Black Mimi, Little Poo, Alice and Harry,
Lovie and Dovie, Thumper and Flopsie,
Tippie, Walter Pigeon, Jake, Velvet.

All those relatives, mostly dry and already
dusty themselves when they returned to the
dust, courtesy of time and Topeka. My father,
with his great faith; my brother injured and
sad; and soon my mother, oblivious to all
but the next dose of morphine.

I mark time since she has stopped eating
and drinking. The hospice nurse avoids
my gaze and tells of a client who lived on
for thirty-eight days at this stage. How is
this possible? Then I remember that we all
live on, in some fashion.

"We are sheep," asserts the nursing home
pastor (as in shepherd) as he begins to read
the 23rd Psalm. But I, unwilling to be lumped
with the simpletons, interrupt with my howl that
some of us are more sheep-like than others.

Classmates, neighbors, colleagues, the
stranger at the bus stop, the shopper in
the check-out line, the local TV personality,
the ethically-challenged politician. Here we
have formed our (yes) flock in this place.

Topeka has given me all of them and
consumed them all back like tiny delicacies
briefly savored, or craw-sized chunks hard
to digest. They muddle around now as
ashes, or dirt, air or bacteria or sunlight
until they find their own equilibrium in the
cosmos, unaware of the life support I provide
in my remembrances, their occasional encore.

To know this, to have steadfastly loved and
tempered the concussions and truncations, I
draw from a leaky reservoir of courage
and welcome this new day, as I plan another
funeral in Topeka.

No one pretended
it was a
fair fight

When Lizards Dream

When lizards dream, is there
a habeas corpus, a gypsy
moth, a climax? Is there some
hot stud of a salamander with
his ballistic tongue a-flicking,
that awakens in a swirling heap
of musty sad leaves getting
staler by the minute, as he tries
to remember the last time he
slithered across a busy highway
for love?

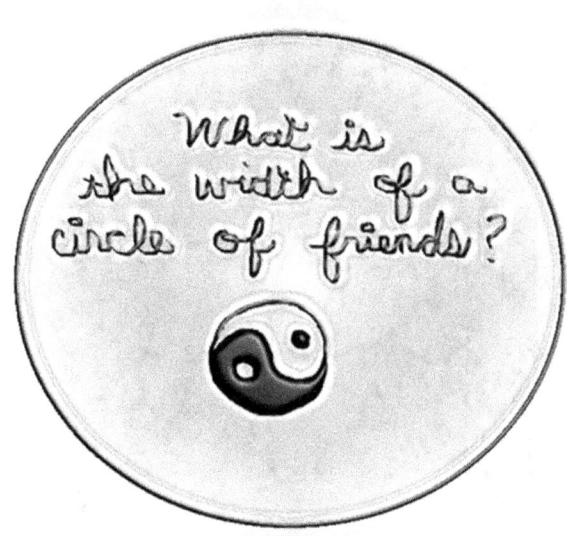

A Tart's Rouge *

Young beanpoles, chasing the learning curve of a tart's rouge.
All fluttery and come hither, encouraged by a tart's rouge.

Bright hopes, brighter lipstick, burning up those first kisses.
Love—ain't it grand?—if only with yourself in a tart's rouge.

What is the turning point when the gloss becomes a crutch?
You, too sharp, too shiny, in danger of becoming a tart's rouge.

Someday you may relax in your own face, discerning and sure,
as you laugh at mirrors from too many good times in a tart's rouge.

Those little brushstrokes called life, earning the face you deserve.
Maybe it should have been sunscreen all along, not a tart's rouge.

Plenipotentiary Poker   *

I'm not especially appreciative of Coolidge's anthropomorphic initiative (the one of dogs with cards around the table) because if dogs were really inclined to this level of vice they wouldn't be nearly as nice. Nevertheless, I confess the work has a quirky appeal. So let's pretend it's real.

"Deal me in," I'll say, though I can never understand what makes a good poker hand. But I'll have the advantage anyway, because man's best friend has too many "tells." Like frantic whimpering spells, machine gun thumping of tails, the bring-your-own-towel foaming and drooling, and savage cushion chewing. And they're certainly hard-wired to obey. "Call, raise, or check!" I'll demand with authority and just watch that pack's conformity.

Most of them ante with Alpo, not money, sometimes resulting in somebody gulping the entire pot, which gets snapped at a lot. As recompense, I'll stand the expense of extra kibble and feed the kitty so things don't get untenable.

As to where will the mutts be fitting those tails as they're sitting on chairs? After a few beers nobody cares. Yes, there's frustration in the collaboration. But sportsmanship states I forget all that, learn poker etiquette, and study the straights and flushes, blinds and full houses. So what if dogs can't bluff? I will play the game with its draws and studs, bitches, hounds, and pooches, and that will be enough.

And if human smell completely overwhelms our little poker den, I'll go roll in something rotten, then come back to the game again.

Whitey's Bar

You took me to our favorite, sordid, red-
neck bar that day in the rain, not
caring that the umbrella hit my head.
(I was too tall and rain would spot
your beautiful leather jacket, you said.)
Inside, with a façade of constrained class,
the mounted deer head gave me the eye
from his fly-specked wall. Did he laugh,
I wonder, or cry, as you tore out my
heart and placed it next to the empty glass?

I was brave—will you listen to me?—
two tears and mascara when you
murmured, "Good things come to me
when I'm cool." But the rain knew
your sophistry and muttered in sympathy.

These are the laws of Whitey's when
one loves too much. Another drink
would have helped, or a gut-punch. Can
I tell you the deer head winked?
But you drove me home then.

Tranquility Base   *
July 20, 1969
To N.A.

They should have sent a poet with us scientists. But the Mission's success is far too critical to leave in non-technical hands and no computational plan would accommodate an additional man.

    As long as night has torn the peaceful sweet of day,
    and orb of ghostly light pulled time and tide along its way,
    that long have fools and sages pondered why
    the step-child moon menaces world and sky.

Before engineering and flight school I studied history. Sailors, shepherds, cavemen, kings, all subject to this moon. No one's ever been immune.

    So ancient souls bemoaned its hazen rings,
    omen of tempests, torments, born of godless things.
    Its blood-red face foretold in prophecy,
    apocalyptic star-cursed tragedy.

Affirmative. Poet imperative. But I am the one who has to convey the historic importance of today.

    Yet this, the moment, now dispels our dread,
    undoing doubts we've wailed as prophets bled.
    To tame the sterile rock as was designed
    I take One Giant Leap for all mankind.

Must rehearse that "Giant Leap" verse. Brainwork of some pedant on the payroll. Now it's all political.

    A leap unmatched by legions' swollen ranks
    when continents lay leveled in their tracks.
    This chasm breached by stepping to the sky;
    my mortal footprint firm in Heaven's eye.

When the moon-a hits your eye like a big-ga pizza pie . . .

    "Houston, Tranquility Base here. The Eagle has landed."

Cultivation

You throw down words on pages,
acres of creamed peas,
mostly mush.

Then, a small poppy appears
and you marvel, surrendering
gladly, sadly to this addiction.

Maybe Take A Stand

Climbing the volcano and other extremes,
shuffling fake news and raspberry creams,
watching the minutes away, tick-tocking
like some coward's pale knees, knocking.
Never thin or rich enough, but medicated,
too clean or way dirty, protein sated.
But vegan in the end
for the planet's sake, Friend,
or a cameo of someone else standing in.

Crusoe, On The Verge

*Some speck afar on the ocean. I will light a signal fire ere
rains and savages return.*

Could I be but clad in clean and proper finery,
woven by the hand of another,
this feverish contagion in my head would be little insolent.
Though I fear it will take more than a bit
of silk and a few pearl buttons to—

Look—the rains conspire beyond the cliff. An omen, surely.—

God's heart I should swear, in spite of my superior cunning
I be half-crazy now, aye, crazy enough,
lamenting the lost comforts of civilization,
an English voice, a tankard of ale,
a warm feather bed.
None in His Majesty's service be more desirous of these items
than I—

*—I resume this missive now, after a fright. Only a
stray peccary, but vicious and wily in its intentions—*

—for none has endured their absence so keenly.
A perdition, the place. Island of Despair.
How could I have divined years ago
when I left a wanderer
that I would end a Pilgrim, ever waiting
for salvation? Twenty-eight years, two months, and nineteen days.
Waiting
for the tide to bring its creatures for my net and spear. Waiting
for the infernal rains to stop,
for the rotting of leaf and flesh and mind to cease.
Watchful for the return of the heathen cannibals who would
skin me and fix
my sightless head on their pole,

dine on my thin old bones
with no good Christian prayer for my soul's redemption.
By Almighty God can it be real vellum under my quill—
the stuff of a proper log to record the misfortune and faith
of these days?
No.
I be delusional.
Yet still I will write,
though it be only wet sand in which I scribe—

*—that speck afar there on the ocean, perhaps
a bit closer?—*

—and all labors erased too soon
by time and tide.

M. H.

Mother House:
Monastic halcyon
Merciful haven
Mortal humans
Mostly holy
(maybe half
mild headache)
Model humility
Maidenly honor
Modest habits
Musical hymns
Myopic homilies
Mystical high
Much healing
Mission's hope
Mary's heart
Manifests here
Many heavenly
Miracles happen.

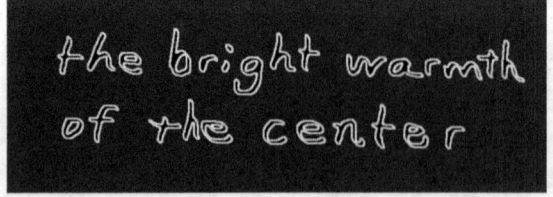

Stay by My Cradle, Please

The large Baby Jesus soldiered on
in the crèche's manger on the Lutheran lawn,
where congregants gathered for Christmas goodwill
and Peace on Earth seemed possible, still.

But Wednesday, some miscreant sinner for fun,
mowed down The Three Kings with a short-barreled gun.
"Oh Christ," swore the janitor under his breath.
"What nut-job shoots Paper Mache to death?"

The church's faith, once incorruptible,
split over the high insurance deductible.
So next year, defending an ancient fable,
an armed guard will stand watch over the stable.

Illegals

While Congress and bigots were busy debating
illegal immigration and agitating
for a xenophobic border wall,
the question was settled once and for all
as *real* aliens from a faraway starry
galaxy just east of Alpha Centauri
invaded the planet and took control
of our over-warmed world and future dust bowl.

Some Earthlings considered it all for the good,
but others hissed, "There goes the neighborhood."

Brexit

When tribal leaders voted a cease-fire
the moated island natives didn't care. They
savored pounding down some feral enemy
and scalping their (mostly) figurative E.U. hair.

Suspicion dies hard. That's why borders make
commercial bloodshed archipelagos of pride
and lands amass great periodic outbreaks
of stink-eye cast at anyone outside.

If France delivered croissants, the Netherlands
produced great cheese, and England's cost of
living went hand-in-hand with all Spain's
plethora of ham, would most folks be
hard to appease?

And would that, perhaps, bring Brexit
to its knees?

Homage

I made the graveyard pilgrimage to see
the old New England plot, the grave of Emily.
An iron fence around the stone held sway
in keeping all admirers away,
but didn't stop ecstatic "Wild Nights" quotes
or scribbled praises left on many grass-stained notes.

I was a young girl then and quite obsessed,
so went there hoping my verse could be judged and blessed.
As if her simple greatness could be found
and passed from some cold oracle in the ground,
to lend my work her authenticity
and stroke the hopeful feathers of my vanity.

But the Belle of Amherst held her secrets dear
and spoke no word of her instructions in my ear.
She was to such requests as mine immune,
consigned to Immortality that afternoon.
I left the grave and never went again,
although I still write poems every now and then.

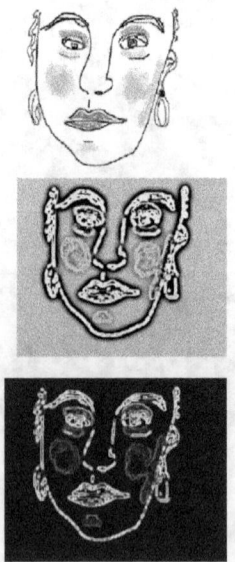

The Lot Sent to Munich   *

"Possibly some of the missing fragments of the skulls in Cope's collection, now in the American Museum, may be in the lot sent to Munich, and vice versa."
—Charles H. Sternberg, *Life of A Fossil Hunter*, about his 1895 expedition

You live a complete life; then you die. After

        millions of years you find
yourself in the Texas breaks near Grey Creek in
Mr. Craddock's pasture, reduced to fragmentary
specimens in a bone bed carried by floods into a
narrow gulch, concreted into sward and sediment
as limbo cushions you from the unimportance
of your nullification. (Did you ever matter to your
fellow *naosaurus clavigers?* Though I suppose
even a giant fin-backed lizard had a mother.) Some

        bipedal creature that never
existed during your lifetime comes along with a pick
and an obsession. "Here little bones," he calls.
"Precious bones. Sweet bones. Where are you?" As
if something called money could be worth any part of
you. Your communion with eons and ages endures a
brief interruption then, relatively speaking. Still, it's a

        resurrection. Not life, exactly, but
a pardon, the patient, meticulous strokes of soft brushes
and careful mallets compelling death to surrender you
from the casket of Mr. Craddock's evolving pasture. Will

        we all be thusly dusted off some day
by a being we won't recognize, our lots sent to New York,
or Munich, or Heaven, like sweet bony freight? How does
it feel, I wonder, when eternity has an

        addendum? It was discovered that
none of the narrow gulch's fragments could be reassembled
into a perfect skull.

The Garden

My garden holds a slender perfect rose,
intoxicating, delicate and sweet—
condemned to fade as surely as it grows.

No unavailing gardener could compose
to set a meaner trap of such conceit:
my garden holds a slender perfect rose,

whose tenderness will die with winter's snows,
whose petals wilt in August's brutal heat,
condemned to fade as surely as it grows.

With time all that's sublime will juxtapose
into the careless compost of deceit.
My garden holds a slender perfect rose.

The earth brings every life form to a close;
the heaven in every rose dies incomplete,
condemned to fade as surely as it grows.

But oh, perennial bloom, the season shows
some things must fade in order to repeat.
My garden holds a slender perfect rose,
condemned to fade as surely as it grows.

Cat Tale

She has a black housecat the size
of Sasquatch and twice as hairy.
At night the cat and his protective
sister, also black, sandwich
her between them in the bed,
warm bologna cuddled
by two purring pumpernickels.

Sometimes in the mornings she
awakes and finds a dampish toy
delivered to her pillow, the devolved
hunter's treat of a single dying rat,
hold the mustard.

Each Life Could Be

Each life could be a movie,
flexing and galumping at a
deadening pace and too
arbitrary a length for the
Fat Plot.

We all want to be Princess
Somebody or Hero Ironperson.
But some of us founder at the
escarpments or gas chambers
or tar babies.

Still, like circumspect butterflies
in a prismatic field, we flicker on
in our role, playing for the cosmic
academy award, not so much a
prize as a breathless woundless
Intermission.

When The Aliens Finally Reveal Themselves

When the aliens finally reveal themselves, undeniably,
irrefutably, I will be folding socks and underwear
and you will be fingering the cantaloupes at Shop Cool,
or pawning the silver tea service, or having your
appendix out.

When The Big One chooses to quake, blasting
and flexing its capricious megamuscle, I will be
wiping spittle from my baby's little mouth and you
will be spinning microbes in the centrifuge, or digging
a window-well in hardpan clay, or filling out tax forms.

When the end of the Anthropocene Age whimpers, I
will be grinding rhinoceros horn into male enhancement
potions and you will be changing a tractor tire, or
performing Rachmaninoff's Piano Concerto 2, or shopping
for dusty rose shag carpeting for the den.

There will be a few puzzling moments as the brain resets
to a new paradigm:
Do we break out the arsenal stockpiled in the basement?
Gather the congregation and pray? Get crazy high
and loot the electronics store? Too many choices,
or maybe none, with seconds counting down.

I will leave off the pairing of socks then, and you
with your cantaloupes, concertos, and carpets, your
cloisters and cannonballs, will have to figure out
by yourself if it was fun and if, in the end, it was
worth it.

Throwaway People
who clutter our lives,
tossed-aside husbands,
discarded wives,
by-gone acquaintances,
casual friends,
countless ex-lovers
and one-night stands,
relatives outgrown,
neighbors ignored,
—why is it
they leave us
restless and bored?
Crumbs of relationships,
never the whole.
Life's expectations
that somebody stole.
Deeds unforgiven,
no pardon revives.
Loveless, we squander
our throwaway lives.

The Guardian
To S.A.

The train used to stop in Wakarusa.
Bloated from sucking dusty plains
it would pause there to belch out its cargo,
wilted cabbages in limp dresses and stiff bonnets,
scowling patriarchs,
parsons,
or politicians,
passengers who, from having to be there or nowhere,
came to the Wakarusa Hotel,
the crucible of Kansas,
custodian of souls and seasons.

There were trees shading it then,
cottonwoods,
like those along the riverbank.
Tall, catching the wind,
broad leaves spinning mosaics
of shadow and light on the limestone.

Such square walls, that hotel.
Denied imported marble or gaudy granite.
Limestone.
Millions of sea creatures millennia ago
sedimented themselves
for the sake of those walls.

Walnut timbers, solid and true,
felled from distant groves,
hauled,
shaped,
hoisted overhead.

Valentine

Strong, square-headed nails,
pounded,
angled,
cursed into place.
Mortar and muscle and dreams.

So that farm hands, fresh with new brides,
could make babies on their wedding nights,
grandmothers could dip their hankies into cool well water,
travelers, midway to somewhere,
could take a room, pull off their boots,
and sleep snoring,
while close in the prairie's darkness
a barred owl ripped its prey.

One of your ancestors, no doubt,
poses in a museum photo beside his horse and buggy,
scowling since 1873 under the Wakarusa Hotel marquee.

Scowling, you set your jaw and bought the damned old place.
Vacant now. Roof caved in.
Birds' nests and black snakes everywhere.
To fix up, you said, to live in.
To add skylights and dual shower heads for water sports,
a chain-link fence,
a humidifier.

Never knowing
that you're the guardian.
Dispossessed lineage of sea creatures, forests, dreams,
ghosts of souls and savages,
babies you will conceive.
Or why you will sleep restless there
as the barred owl patiently
endures.

The Blue Potomac Waltz

Once I also courted you, my worldly
prince, a little waltz in three-fourths time,
pearls and Camelot, you know, the pearls
as in "don't cast your pearls before swine."
Swine or swain it's all the same. A waltz
is merely frosting on your repertoire,
the pearls congealed and Camelot got lost
somewhere: King Arthur but no Guinevere.
The Blue Potomac Waltz, da da da Dum,
de Dum, de Dum, but strummed in castoff chords,
subdued platonic waltz, a dance whose outcome
drowned a fragile bluesy score.

Pinkie

The hole in the sock,
the size a big clue,
the sock on the foot
you've slipped out of your shoe.

The hole in the sock,
a phalangeal review;
such getting-to-know-you
is long overdue.

The hole in the sock,
the sock on the floor.
Let's peel off your other sock
and close the door.

Native Stone

Having grown up in New York City she wore
cowboy boots and turquoise jewelry to appear as if
from Albuquerque.

She told me about being raped without crying out,
how black people in red wigs murdered on the subway,
the air fetid and dirty.

How private schools became fortresses to keep
education in but seldom kept ignorance out.
Four o'clock one morning

a man in a trench coat almost shot her
just because. She said it was cold.
Biggest sun warming

alfalfa fields is how I remember Kansas, I said.
Driving the tractor hard in low gear. Hay in
big round bales before winter.

Scalding headless chickens forty at a time.
Run your hand against the grain of the feathers, that way
they come off better.

Corn prices down and root worms bad this year.
Shuck a half-bushel of roastin' ears for the
covered dish supper.

Big clean clouds in a blue-clean sky until
a gullywasher battered the crops but brought
good fishing weather.

Four in the morning, one hour of sleep before
time to milk. All done by machine now.
Cows don't like cold hands.

That's very interesting, she said. She studies
anthropology and considers Kansas classic Americana.
Can't she understand?

I'm hard as a Kansas fossil. She's never
dirtied her hands castrating pigs.

The Second Time Climbing Teotihuacán   *

Hector drove her the first time in his daddy's car, black
with diplomatic plates. She was seventeen and knew
everything. *Magical Mystery Tour* was her favorite
song, capturing arcing energies and sensual alignments
like an over-exposed photograph.

They climbed that big monster, holding hands for the
steepness, until leaving everything-that-wasn't-magic
behind. At the top the air was thin. There was timelessness,
multiple epiphanies, lustful regenerations. They shared
a cigarette high on the Mexican plateau. Hector *no
hablaba inglés,* but he loved The Beatles.

Some *pinche* chauffeur named Maximiliano, "call me
Max" drove her the second time in his crappy Renault.
She was twenty-seven and knew everything. Her husband
came too, a faltering tourist of insufficient equipoise
seeking antiquities, controlled strangeness. He left no
oddity of The Avenue of the Dead unphotographed,
clicking the shutter, capturing nothing but obligation.

They climbed that big monster on the writ large expanse,
husband a galley oarsman heaving up the steps behind her.
At the top she took in the view, deathless-as-platinum, again
and for the last time, then rasped down a Mexican cigarette,
like after a difficult coitus.

That night she had four Bloody Marys and threw up loudly
in the middle of *La Reforma*. It was the altitude. The husband
consumed countless pastries from the *panadería* and threw up
silently four times in the hotel bathroom. It was the bulimia.
She didn't know anything about that, until then.

Evidence *

For Dark Matter, physicists are quite sure some
exists in the unfingered realm of Kingdom Come,
without evidence from even one Light Matter crumb.

Does it balance rock candy, plaid socks, and smug giraffes?
Does it sweat with the oldies and collect louche photographs?
Will it halt the cold footman who holds my coat and laughs?

But never mind the boffins of science because Dark
Matter remains a whim in a question mark.

Dove Season

Dove Season

Little grey dove, how did you decode
the foreigner's thrumming—*I am so lonely*—
to accept its invitation? It was just a white
plastic bag snared in the maple tree, the
ubiquitous flag of a nation surrendering
to trash, but you perched at its side for hours,
a splendorous lady taking tea with the chateau's
pale host while pretending to admire the tapestries.

When you finally collected your veins and your
feathers, your coos and your flutters, you flew
south and it was over, the puff of your soft exit
the extinguishment of a candle after the party
expires.

But the white bag calls out *Come back!* with its
canon-shot whipping and snapping, its ugly
song of longing immune to uncertain seasons
and their fickle little grey memories.

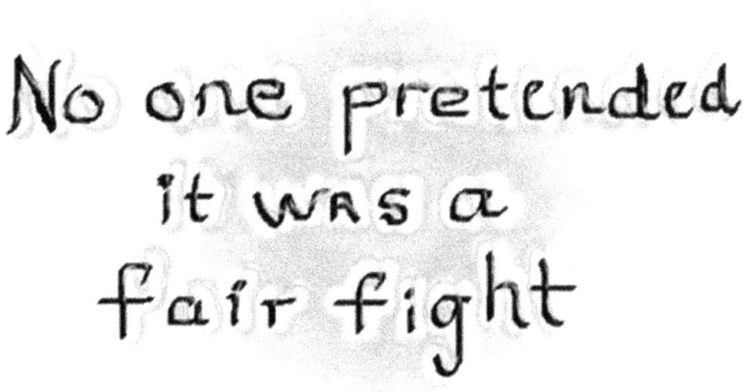

> No one pretended
> it was a
> fair fight

Waking Up Shocking Pink

Another peppermint morning. The color
ga-boinks left and right in her head: all
bubble gum, roses, the blush of flamingoes.
Sanity—tinted—has fled.

She and the chiaroscuro cat dance
curlicues in a four-square room.
But the cat makes a grab for the lead
during a chittering castanet tune.

Outside, a snufbumble snow would bleach
her encore a step out of synch. So
she snaps on her visor from Acapulco,
to howl with the neon, the abracadabra,
the monochromatic cotillion of pink.

Guerrilla Warfare

The cold, hard edges of me
have their own memory of
time when stakes were driven,
blood was let, left to
define those boundaries—
undisturbed straight lines.

A delicate sensibility threatens
now to mutiny—insidious,
serene treachery, lulling
with its soft caresses those
clever, cold, hard edges.

Unthinkable that part of me
should disobey that tyranny
imposed in pain, inscribed in
blood, which promised to keep
out the world.

But world is waiting. Whether
menace or relief, this gentle
side will cause me grief:
some fractured sentimental fool,
too weak to curb emotion,
torn apart, half kind, half cruel.

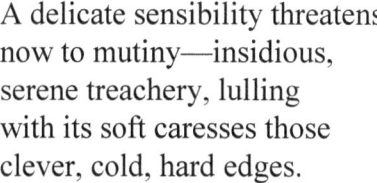

Halloween

As bogeymen claim darkness,
every foraging ghoul
haunts its jaundiced
kingdom, lovingly,
menacingly,
never openly pursuing
quickening, rather,
stealthily tasting
undead viscera,
waylaying
xeric
yummy
zombies.

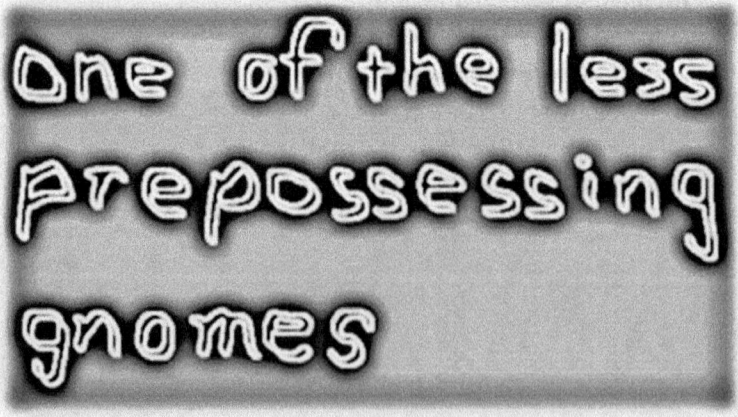

Disclaimer

From shocking pink of passion,
To bloody crimson's lust,
The covenants we fashion
Will oxidize and rust.
Mortality's to borrow,
Most certainly tomorrow
The stains of bliss and sorrow
Go grey from dust to dust.

Spotlight on a Mummer *

This pale bag of energy using my name,
walking around claiming to be a self,
is mostly full of rigidity, decaying
opposable thumbs, and occasionally
something original, aboriginal, and
boundless. As in part of a bigger glory.
Modern physics pins down the current
nature of reality, but what information,
like fairy dust, do the scholars bring to
bear on my life when the alarm goes off
in the a.m.? Cunning and pity, all a
dream, butter on the bread we choose to
eat. Shall we pluck up courage to move
at least one molecule, or make a covenant
with a butterfly—the one in South
America whose impact ripples on and on?

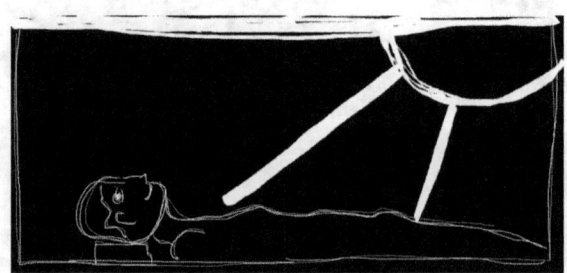

Blue Bandage

The Polish History class was halfway through
when, laying out the task for peer review,
a classmate yanked her shirt up to expose
the wrapped blue bandage underneath her clothes.

We stared enthralled as she, without a word,
glared at the bandage, flushed yet undeterred,
until the reaching of some weighty mass
(perhaps The Vasa Dynasty in class)
had tipped the scales to just the right ideal:
the perfect moment for The Big Reveal.

I think the monarchy of Stanislaw
was when she ripped that bandage like a saw.
And there it was, the gruesome purple wound,
much worse than what we peasants had assumed.

We quickly looked away, our own Dark Ages,
afraid the blueness of it was contagious.

Ruth Maus

Allen Ate the Earring

Allen ate the earring,
not because he was hungry,
but because he was a Terrible
Two and fixated on the shiny
razzamatazz with turquoise
florettes and deadly screw-on back.

He only ate one. Perhaps
it wasn't tasty enough for
seconds,
or maybe the little omnivore
got caught before more coveting.

Stuff him with bread and
mashed potatoes, the doctor said.
He had seen this before.

After many years the earrings
and matching bracelet have passed
—so to speak—
to Allen's sister, but she neither
wears them
nor eats them.

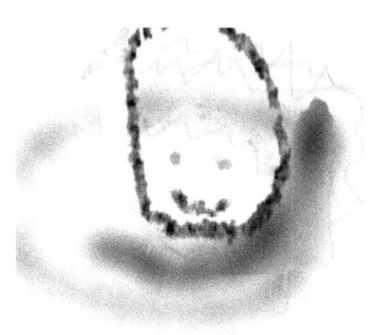

The Brother

A massive brain hemorrhage, said the coroner.
Two days undiscovered in his bed.
We broke into the house, how inconvenient.
The frumpy pillow shivering in red.

A nightstand radio aimlessly playing.
I blotted out the words until the song
Something something crushing with a hammer,
Asking *where had all the flowers gone?*

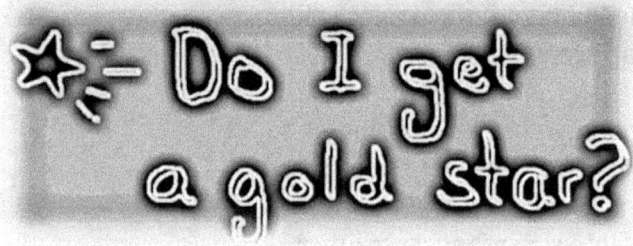

To Sit Around Fires

There is this lulling that incapacitates your
ability for speech into a
sweet spot of heart
and hurt.
Against the sizeable distrust of
dark, the
orange-blue warms you with its writhing
and spitting of spells to
unknown totems.

That you, a cosmic rookie, should receive
this blessing
after
all your transgressions,
is to grasp at the balm that perhaps
there will be a new day
after all.

It Depends On Your Perspective

I'm Possum, rather coarse and slight.
My fur is grey; I hunt at night.
Marsupial and omnivore,
with subterfuge that most abhor.

You see I'm many species' prey
and much too slow to run away,
so if I wish to stay alive,
I must "play possum" to survive.

This process mimics my demise
as gasping, I roll back my eyes,
convulse and twitch and urinate
and vomit the last meal I ate,
then make my anal glands expel
a horribly offensive smell.

My tactics, which on close review
will make you want to vomit too,
repel quite nicely those who'd be
a Possum's natural enemy.

I know some humans' fur is grey.
Your species mostly hunts by day.
You think your big brain makes you wise,
however, you don't realize

the thousand ways you play the fool,
act gross, and invite ridicule,
or see how uncouth you can get
—when there's no predator or threat.

My Possum's ruse results from fear
as evolution has made clear.
But you behave much like we do,

oblivious, as you stink too,
that in humiliation's throes
your shameful mess was one you chose.

Thus, while our species both affect
to treat ourselves with disrespect,
Possums have motive; you have none.
So which beast is the clever one?

Hurricane Dance

The season knows a gale of crashing force,
collision course of pressures, energized
by men who use their might without remorse,
by women, prickly comrades, calcified.
When will the revolutions stabilize?
When will calm follow hurricane's disaster?
I wait for the barometer to rise,
but nature doesn't indicate an answer.

So waiting out the storm a single dancer,
propelled by powers indifferent to applause,
pivots from unsynchronized romancers.
Oh lovely women, handsome men: because
a *pas de deux*, precise, requires delicacy,
the one who loves me best, for now, is me.

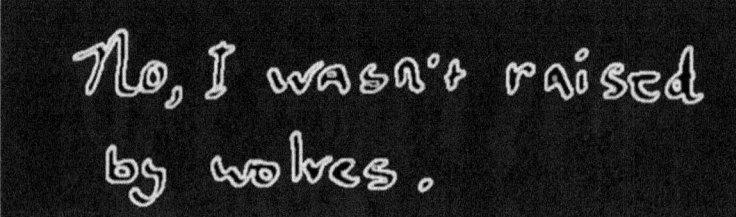

Or Possibly the Queen of Lazy

The woman known as The Princess of
Unfinished Business,
diminished by her insistence
on "getting to it later,"
might also have been labeled (aside from
the sugarcoating, euphemism, understatement,
public relations spin, and other terms
I hope to research someday)
as a procrastinator,
for instance.

Poem for Poetry Geeks

With poems I have a rendezvous;
I didn't mean to, but I do.
My own poems—they just don't flow,
a fate all English majors know,
compared to the sublime excess
as *how do I love thee*'s coalesce,
and ravens quoth and brigades die,
where roads diverge in a wood, and I
have water, water everywhere,
but don't go gentle anywhere.
And still I rise where sidewalks end,
and lonely clouds are my best friend.
A loaf of bread, a jug of wine,
a summer's day, a pick-up line,
soon love is like a red, red rose
and two if by sea, I suppose.
Then there's the Jabberwocky song;
it howls a bit, though I was wrong
that coy mistress was a sham,
for Mary had a little lamb (to go with her green eggs and ham.)
So now I'm captain of my soul
and know full well for whom bells toll.
That's why, wild nights instead of thee,
I wrap myself in poetry.
In doing so I do not sleep.
I take to the open road; I weep.
I walk in beauty, like the night
and sail a pea-green boat in spite
of life, with loveliness to sell,
and seven circles just for hell.
There Grecian urn, Calico Cat,
and mighty Casey at the bat
sing odes to nightingales for years,
then part in silence and in tears,
while Gunga Din—may his tribe increase—

and Agamemnon and his niece
play Lady of Shallot till dawn
then go where Simon's pieman's gone,
between the crosses, row on row,
like weeds, as country churchyards go.

It's never been more clear to me,
in such praiseworthy company,
I think that I shall never see
a Nobel Prize for poetry.

The Convenience Store Clerk

The young man wore his misery as a skin.
More than the taxidermy for his meat,
it was the impasse of his cells, the glue-grip
of his respirations. It was his cardboard voice
accusing "What do you want?" and the
intravenous mud transfused and slow-dripped
throughout some fingernail-hanging life.

The customers purchased some BBQ chips and
a lottery ticket, but no one would touch the
shriveled hot dogs.

Parts of A Hen

The Mother Hen's job description reads "fussing and things
like that." She hovers over the idiot little ones, so many,
gathering them ("Here, babies, here!") under her wings
like a feathered Sherman tank full of Peeps. If any
one will profane your name it's The Wet Hen, so you
don't cross her, even dry, for she's fowl-tempered at best.
Then there's The Chick. Hot stuff, hubba hubba, and hoot-
chie cootchie! Sadly, one day she grew a ravishing breast,
fell for some foreign rooster (a Jersey Giant?), and became
the aforementioned Mother, a plight she realized
when the eggs began to hatch. The Alarmist, a.k.a.
Chicken Little of ". . . sky is falling!" fame, gets the prize
for most media exposure. I think she invented this genre,
along with her friend and accomplice Henny Penny who
was always running to tell the king some great problem.
Of course most of the time it just wasn't true.
The Biddy, if she lives long enough to become one,
is another unpopular, godmother hen. Still, she serves
an important role, a target on which to vent our frustration
because she's so shrill and busybodyish, so she deserves
her own merit in the hierarchy. One of my
favorites is The Dumb Cluck, (the dumb blonde
of the poultry family) because she fries
up so well and there's more than enough to go around.

The Pusher

There is an elderly woman with my mother's name in the nursing home, infirmities and dementia switching out body and mind like in *Invasion of the Body Snatchers*, an unrecognizable person in place of someone familiar. I look at the wheelchair and the bandages, pay the medical bills and consult with the doctors, but I picture Frances in her 1950s and 60s prime, The Titan of Tupperware.

Tupperware's legal plastic kitchen containers and utensils sported come-hither names like Vent 'N Serve and Square Round (which was, in fact, square), providing suburban homemakers like Mom somewhere to store leftover tuna casseroles, practicality being next to godliness in the catechism of girdled women who ached in their hearts to be Betty Crocker (who was, in fact, fictitious.) It was the perfect muscatel for a muslin market.

In Mom's hands, Tupperware transmutated into something more like holy water, baptizing her kitchen and her apron-clad life with Betty's cheerfulness and efficiency as she stored cereal, bread, crackers, and bacon in their proper upright or oblong containers. This pleasure, like most outrageous bliss in short supply to housewives, demanded more. So she became a dealer, pushing the products to others to make money, so she could get more Tupperware.

She came from a long line of pushers. The nuns had pushed her into fear of non-conformity; her parents pushed her to decline the college scholarship she won as valedictorian. Society pushed her into marriage to that sailor home from the war, into having four babies, and into a white-gloves-hat-and-matching-purse-and-shoes existence. Some primal sweet tooth of emptiness and appetite pushed her to become creative.

Our living room smelled like bergamot, like *Evening In Paris* during those 1950s evenings in Kansas as Mom began hosting her Tupperware parties there. Bright lights illuminated products while card-table folding chairs held as many flamboyantly perfumed ladies as possible. Gabfests with the girls, those sweater-setted or shirtwaisted young wives, teachers, and secretaries, a cotton-candy introduction to a lifetime of costly neediness. Laughing and passing around cupcakes frosted with rainbow confetti sprinkles, tart yellow lemon bars, "party favors" of Tupperware products of all shapes, sizes, colors, and purposes so you can touch them and smell them, snap the lids on and off, on and off, imagine becoming Betty.

The dollars flowed uphill as Mom blossomed into a flag-waving pusher – – – savvy and friendly, with an encyclopedic repertoire of hostess party games and her own Tupperware habit that slammed downhill on us. We absorbed Cake Takers, Wonderlier Bowl 3-piece Sets, and Jel-ette Molds as we ate mountains of green gelatin with fruit cocktail and orange gelatin with slivered carrots, crushed pineapple, and miniature marshmallows.

An extra room appeared on our house, with new shelves, cupboards, and closets where the stuff multiplied overnight, like the sorcerer's apprentice conjuring tempera-colored potions of pink, blue, green, or harvest gold plastic. The folly was *trying to find the matching lid,* with so many ovoids, squares, and round flat discs fitting a tiny Midget up to a Godzilla-sized Thatsa Mega Bowl. Mom's old grey Studebaker was replaced by a huge blue station wagon with plenty of cargo room and an engine like a canon, loud and sure of itself as Mom mobilized her pushing into surrounding counties.

The road show's scariest item was the Crisp-It Lettuce Keeper, which Mom introduced to audiences as the perfect size and configuration to hold a head. Of lettuce. Its verdant roundness came with an impressive Taj Mahal-like raised dome on the lid and large green plastic spike on which to violently impale its contents.

Sometimes we pushed back at Mom, half-joking that when she died we would cram her into a Tupperware coffin, burp it (to get the air out) and seal it with its matching lid. There she would remain airtight and waterproof for eternity, since Tupperware wouldn't chip, crack, break, or peel, and if it were defective we could return it within 30 days for a free replacement.

In fact, some of it *was* defective. We now know many of those early Tumblers and Servalier One Touch Canister sets contained polycarbonate Bisphenol A (BPA). But the neighborhood pushers, with their license to help eager women store and preserve deviled eggs and half-eaten pies, were not chemists or environmental scientists, were not to blame for whatever ugliness may have leeched into the lunch meat.

Tupperware and Mom reinforced each other's needs and energy in the way these sorts of attachments do. She pushed her product in the evenings so that during the day she could pack my Roy Rogers and Trigger school lunch pail with bologna sandwiches, potato chips, and a thermos of whole milk. She decreed the indispensability of swimming lessons, piano lessons, and choir practice, served as Girl Scout troop leader, held flash cards of multiplication tables for our memorization, and spanked thems that needed spankin'. She sat down and learned Braille, then taught it to my severely and permanently disabled brother, helping him navigate the botched-up world while his Talking Books and tape recorder captured some of the Tupperware shelving, and his vulnerabilities captured everything else.

When it came time, she assisted three of my great-aunts through their final illnesses, handling their estates with the financial proficiency she had learned calculating Tupperware invoices and commissions. She cared for my father as he lay dying, emptying his ostomy bags, changing soiled sheets in the middle of the night, giving her husband of sixty-two years the same diligence she had given her customers.

In her business Mom won prizes and cash bonuses and became a manager over other dealers. But even after she retired, after there were no more hostess parties to schedule, no more national Tupperware conventions to attend, no more dealers to recruit, the center of gravity of her home remained her accumulation of Tupperware products, a dense hedgerow of thorns and memories which confronted me after her hospitalization. I selected a Kaliopi Serving Bowl with its florescent pink lid to hold her cremains. The rest I destroyed, the stash the survivor flushes away when their loved one enters a twelve-step program. The product is perfectly safe now, just not safe for me.

Now I push a few poems and wait for my mother's death, her body's death. Wait for the tumors and the sores and the winking-out synapses to do their job, for the phone call from hospice.

We have already lost Frances, a chatty blonde with poufy teased hair and out-of-style glasses—crazy smart and mostly kind. But the push of that personality will not be destroyed as easily as the products. It endures in my own determination and (hopefully) kindness, absorbed over a lifetime from the everyday high priestess who fashioned a kingdom out of plastic, habituating herself, her family, and hundreds of drudged-out housewives to the bliss of that unobtainable dream.

Todd rode by *

on his skateboard today.
He was all flash and spandex,
Warhol's *Marilyn Diptych* neoning
on his t-shirt, not real clean,
but still somebody reminiscent
of Peter Parker.

"Hey, man!" I called.
"Can't stop now," he yelled back.
 "Maybe later."

He zoomed by, noticed
the pothole in the road
too late, and flew through
the air with a certain grace
I could only describe
as spider-like.

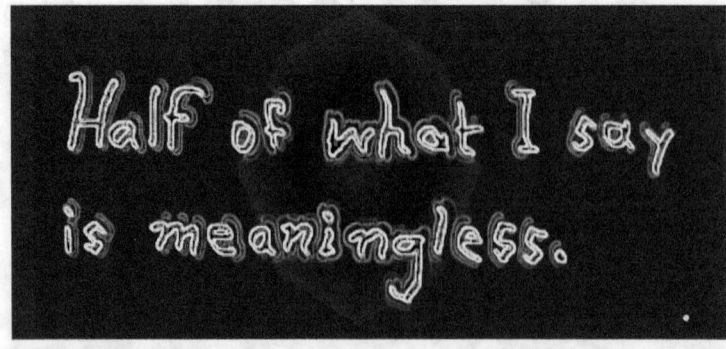

Valentine *

And look what happens
when you can't look me in the eye:
how carefully your hand pares the apples
for your first gift to me, a pie.
Because, after all that paring, you
who can barely cook,
would have to hand me
your heart as well, if you should look.

Ars (Not Quite) Poetica   *

Simply put, a poem should be
an unexpected pregnancy,
a tickle you mistake for gas
until it swallows you *en masse*.

Poems that go trilling in meter and rhyme,
breed ear-worms that pester us all for some time.

Or free verse, thoughts or fragments that
stagger around the
piece, utilizing
indiscriminate line breaks before
making, eventually (or I
should say
hopefully), a
point.

There once was a lecherous poet,
who try as she would to forego it,
      composed innuendo
          right through the crescendo.
And now she's the new Poet Laureate.

Publishing is hard.
Poets must grasp the beauty
of life without cash.

I think that I shall never see
a poem as lovely as a poem written by me.

Here are some rules to assist
if in writing poetry you persist:

          reasons not to forego punctuation are myriad
          so don't do that period

Using clichés in poetry at all
is like banging your head against a brick wall.

Some poems employ profanity and shit
that's rarely of any benefit.

Writing poems during the day
is okay;
or, you may choose to write
a poem when you can't sleep at night.

Hail trochee! Hail synecdoche!
It's hell parsing out poetry.

If you must write poetry, I recommend
going straight from the beginning to

The End.

NOTES*

Waking In The Pink: is an imitation of Robert Lowell's poem "Waking In The Blue."

Ars Poetica: *Ars Poetica* is Latin for "the art of poetry." Originating with the Greek poet Horace (65-8 BC) it is a poem describing the qualities a poem should have if it is to be a work of art.

Modern Love Story: Gladys Thong was the pseudonym of singer/songwriter Dusty Springfield, used when she did not want to be recognized.

The Center Of It All: is an imitation of Ben Lerner's poem "(The sky is a big responsibility . . .)"

Curriculum Vitae: A *Curriculum Vitae* is a brief account of a person's education, qualifications, and previous experience, typically sent with a job application.

A Tart's Rouge: In the 19th century, *tart* was British slang for "pretty woman." The use evolved into slang for a woman of easy virtue.

Plenipotentiary Poker: *Dogs Playing Poker*, by Cassius Marcellus Coolidge, refers collectively to an 1894 painting, a 1903 series of sixteen oil paintings commissioned to advertise cigars, and a 1910 painting. They have been described as being "indelibly burned into the American schlock subconscious." The original 1894 painting sold in 2015 for over $650,000.

Tranquility Base: The penultimate line in this poem was part of a song, "That's Amore," a major hit for Dean Martin in 1953. It received an Academy Award nomination for best original song of the year but did not win. The poem's last line quotes the actual first words spoken on the moon.

M.H.: Written after seeing the letters M.H. on a kitchen paring knife at the Sisters of Charity of Leavenworth Mother House during a seven day silent meditation retreat.

The Lot Sent to Munich: Kansan Charles H. Sternberg (1850-1943) was a fossil collector and paleontologist during the Bone Wars, a period of ruthless competitive fossil hunting in the Gilded Age. Fossils he collected, including dinosaurs, are in museums around the world.

The Guardian: Wakarusa, Kansas, platted in 1858, was the center of a small farming community and a stop on the Atchison, Topeka, and Santa Fe Railroad. The National Register of Historic Places lists The Wakarusa Hotel as the first business beside the railroad station established there. It enjoyed a flourishing trade for decades but declined with modern railroad and business practices. Today it is the oldest surviving structure in a village of 260 and used as a private residence.

The Second Time Climbing Teotihuacán: Located 25 miles NE of Mexico City and 7,500 feet above sea level, Teotihuacán is a significant ancient archeological complex of unknown origin. The enormous Pyramid of the Moon, third largest pyramid in the world, is 150 feet tall with a base 550 x 490 feet. There are 248 steps to the top. The Avenue of The Dead is two and a half miles long. La Reforma is a major street in downtown Mexico City.

Evidence: The line containing "... *the cold footman who holds my coat and laughs*" references the line "*And I have seen the eternal Footman hold my coat, and snicker.*" from T.S. Eliot's poem "The Love Song of J. Alfred Prufrock."

Spotlight On A Mummer: A *mummer* is an actor in a traditional masked mime, especially of a type associated with Christmas and popular in England in the 18th and early 19th centuries. In modern times it is a person who goes merrymaking in disguise, especially during festivals.

Hurricane Dance: In ballet, a *pas de deux* is a dance duet in which two dancers, typically a male and a female, perform ballet steps together.

Poem For Poetry Geeks: contains or parodies lines from these poems and nursery rhymes
- "I Have a Rendezvous with Death," by Alan Seeger
- "This Be The Verse," by Philip Larkin
- "How Do I Love Thee? Sonnet 43," by Elizabeth Barrett Browning
- "The Raven," by Edgar Allan Poe
- "The Charge of the Light Brigade," by Alfred Lord Tennyson
- "The Road Not Taken," by Robert Frost
- "The Rime of the Ancient Mariner," by Samuel Taylor Coleridge
- "Do Not Go Gentle Into That Good Night," by Dylan Thomas
- "And Still I Rise," by Maya Angelou
- "Where The Sidewalk Ends," by Shel Silverstein
- "I Wandered Lonely As A Cloud," by William Wordsworth
- "Rubaiyat," by Omar Khayyam
- "Shall I Compare Thee To A Summer's Day?" (Sonnet 18), by William Shakespeare
- "A Red, Red Rose," by Robert Burns
- "Paul Revere's Ride," by Henry Wadsworth Longfellow
- "Jabberwocky," by Lewis Carroll
- "Howl," by Allen Ginsberg
- "To His Coy Mistress," by Andrew Marvell
- *Green Eggs and Ham*, by Dr. Seuss
- "Invictus," by William Ernest Henley
- "For Whom the Bell Tolls" (No Man Is An Island), by John Donne
- "Wild Nights – Wild Nights!" (249), by Emily Dickinson

- "Do Not Stand At My Grave and Weep," by Mary Elizabeth Frye
- "Song of the Open Road," by Walt Whitman
- "She Walks In Beauty," by George Gordon Byron
- "The Owl and the Pussycat," by Edward Lear
- "Barter," by Sara Teasdale
- "Inferno," by Dante Alighieri
- "Ode on a Grecian Urn," by John Keats
- "The Duel," by Eugene Field
- "Casey at the Bat," by Ernest Lawrence Thayer
- "Ode to a Nightingale," by John Keats
- "When We Two Parted," by George Gordon Byron
- "Abou Ben Adhem," by Leigh Hunt
- "Agamemmon," by Aeschylus
- "The Lady of Shallot," by Alfred, Lord Tennyson
- "In Flanders Fields," by John McCrae
- "Elegy Written in a Country Churchyard," by Thomas Gray
- "Mary Had A Little Lamb"
- "Jack Sprat Could Eat No Fat"
- "Simple Simon Met A Pieman"

Todd Rode By: is an imitation of Roy Beckemeyer's poem "God Rode By."

Valentine: The opening line of this poem is from a line in Elizabeth Bishop's poem "The Shampoo."

Ars (Not Quite) Poetica: A *troche* (pronounced TROW-key) is a stressed syllable followed by an unstressed one. A *synecdoche* (pronounced sin-ECK-doe-key) is a literary device that refers to a whole as one of its parts.

Valentine

A Note about the Author

Ruth Maus, a native of Topeka, Kansas, has pursued a love of learning around the world, with languages, curiosity, and an appreciation for all beings a constant thread. She represented Smith College at the annual Glasscock Intercollegiate Poetry Contest where past contestants have included James Merrill, Sylvia Plath, Katha Pollit, Mary Jo Salter, James Agee, Frederick Buechner, Kenneth Koch, Donald Hall, William Manchester, Muriel Rukeyser, and Gjertrud Schnackenberg. Her poems have appeared in *Inscape*, *Grecourt Review*, *Lighten Up Online,* and *Orchards Poetry Journal.*

Valentine is her first book of poetry.

She currently lives in Topeka where she writes poems and studies at Washburn University when not teaching animals amazing tricks with which to bore her friends.

Photograph by Bill Stephens.

 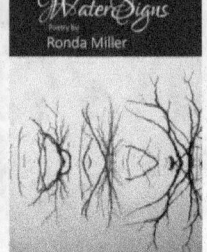  

 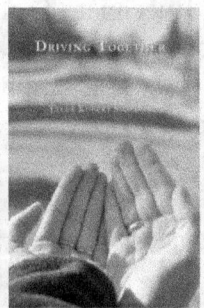  

www.birdypoetryprize.com

Meadowlark Books created The Birdy Poetry Prize to celebrate the voices of this era. Cash prize, publication, and 50 copies awarded annually.

Entries Accepted: May 1 to December 1.

Final Deadline for Entries: December 1, midnight.

Entry Fee: $25

All entries will be considered for standard Meadowlark Books publishing contract offers, as well.

Full-length poetry manuscripts (55 page minimum) will be considered. Poems may be previously published in journals and/or anthologies, but not in full-length, single-author volumes. All poets are eligible to enter, regardless of publishing history.

See the website, meadowlark-books.com, for complete submission guidelines.

Nothing feels better than home

meadowlark-books.com

While we at Meadowlark Books love to travel, we also cherish our home time. We are nourished by our open prairies, our enormous skies, community, family, and friends. We are rooted in this land, and that is why Meadowlark Books publishes regional authors.

When you open one of our fiction books, you'll read delicious stories that are set in the Heartland. Settle in with a volume of poetry, and you'll remember just how much you love this place too—the landscape, its skies, the people.

Meadowlark Books publishes memoir, poetry, short stories, and novels. Read stories that began in the Heartland, that were written here. Add to your Meadowlark Book collection today.

Specializing in Books by Authors from the Heartland Since 2014

www.ingramcontent.com/pod-product-compliance
Lightning Source LLC
Chambersburg PA
CBHW052101070526
44584CB00017B/2288